Everybody Has a Story

The Glory Belongs to God

GLADYS STROTHER WILSON

I must say that I thank God for my story! It is because of Him that I can share my testimony, as I have witnessed His omnipotence. I love the Lord with all my heart and with all that is within me. God has truly been good to me, and for that, I am forever grateful.

Contents

Foreword

Gladys' vulnerability and openness in this book are stunning. Revelation 12:11(KJV) states, "They overcame him by the blood of the Lamb, and by the word of their testimony; and they loved not their lives unto the death." This is the scripture that summarizes Gladys' book. I have known Gladys for over 15 years; since the day I met her, I've witnessed her empower women through her testimony, just as she's enhanced their beauty through hair styling. This book is just an echo of what she has exemplified in her daily living. As you read each testimony, you will become empowered and encouraged to know a God who is genuinely all-powerful and who will bring you through your adversity so that you can share your testimony as well.

The transformation that God has worked within Gladys' life is illustrated through her testimony, as she contrasts her new and old lives. For instance, she shares her experience with drug use, highlighting her previous lack of relationship with God, which ultimately left a void in her life. After encountering God, however, she is transformed into a new creature; she is a tool ready for the Savior's use. She shares how God's spirit, which lives in her, transformed her into the woman she is today.

Based on all that God has done in her life, Gladys urges her readers to open themselves up to a relationship with Christ and to transform, rather than conform to, the pattern of this world (Roman 12:2). Her testimony allows the reader to see that Christ's love is not merely an abstract concept—His love is a way of life. Her story reveals how sharing our testimonies with others can help them see God's love. So, as you read this book, *Everybody Has a Story*, be open, and let others see what God is doing to transform you!

Jacqueline L Goodwin

Founder, Healing in the Vessel Ministries

Introduction

Everybody Has a Story is a true story about the journey of a young girl who experienced the presence of God at an early age. Even though I did not completely understand it, I knew what I felt was real because my mother took me to church every Sunday. God's presence is so real! When I backslid from the things of God, He continued to show up in my life. There were many obstacles that were thrown my way, but they only made me stronger and pulled me closer to Him. Even though God had a plan for my life, it did not stop the fiery darts from coming. The enemy tried his very best to take me out, but God would not allow it.

In this book, you will learn of the emotional and physical abuse I experienced at the hands of my father. I'll share the loneliness and depression I felt but could not speak about, and how I looked for love in the wrong places. There were many hard trials and circumstances that I had to endure to become the woman of God who I am today. God gave me the power to triumph over my troubles. If He did it for me, I know He will do the same for you. There is nothing too hard for my God. He is bigger than all of our problems.

I want to encourage each reader, young and old, to trust God's plan and never give up on life. All He needs is a willing vessel who is not ashamed of the gospel. It does not matter what kind of environment you were reared in or what your past looks like. God can and will use you for His Glory. You do not have to be a product of your environment. Listen to the voice of God; He speaks to you all the time, if you would only listen. My prayer is that God receives the glory from my life through the gift of writing. Please take the time to meditate on the Scriptures that are provided for you. My desire is for you to be drawn closer to Him and to encounter his love and presence through each written page.

God has also inspired me to write and include some of my inner thoughts in the form of poetry, which is included in some of the chapters. I pray that you will experience as much joy reading these words as I did writing them.

Chapter 1

Childhood Beginnings

I t all started when I was just a little girl. I think I was about four years old when I experienced my very first discovery. I remember walking down my grandparents' large, cement steps which led into their kitchen. I remember it so vividly, as if it happened yesterday. It was my first memory of being alive! I felt so happy and free. When I look back, I know it was God's presence that was with me. That's right–I could not explain it, but I knew that God loved me and His presence was forever around me.

The Bible speaks of bringing your child up in the right way, and my parents were sticklers for that. My father did not attend church, but he made certain that I did. It did not matter what was happening in our lives, going to church with my mother every Sunday was necessary. As the Canton Spirituals wrote, "Mama drugged me to church." My mother also made certain that I participated in Sunday school, the choir, the revivals, and both the Easter and Christmas programs. We often traveled with our pastor and his wife to various programs after church on Sunday afternoons.

When we did not have a ride to church, which was most of the time, we would have to walk up a big hill to get there. I believe that this is where I developed a love for nature. The beautiful blue sky, tall trees, and colorful leaves mixed with sunshine were just so lovely to me. Even now, nature is still a peaceful space for me and makes me feel closer to God. I just love when the wind brushes up against my face. It is so refreshing!

I see the wind as it moves upon the leaves, causing a nice little breeze.

It feels so refreshing inside, a feeling I could not hide.

As the vision in front of me would soon come to an end,

I turned around and stared again.

I continued to walk forward as I gazed backward,

mesmerized by God's beautiful creation.

All I could do was smile.

There were times when I felt so tired, but my love for church outweighed those feelings. I would quickly take on any role that was placed before me. I would even travel with the Jubilee Choir to help them sing when they did not have enough members present. It did not bother me to sing with the senior citizens, because I always had a special spot in my heart for them. It felt great to be involved in the house of God, even though I did not really understand it all. I had so much joy in serving God and others. That was good enough for me.

I was baptized for the first time at the age of twelve. I was so nervous, because I didn't know how to swim. I had some crazy thoughts going through my head. I felt better when I saw my pastor holding the noses of the others who went before me. After everything I had learned about Jesus Christ, I knew it was the right thing to do. And all my friends were getting baptized, too.

Childhood Beginnings

Chapter 2

The Only Little Girl

eing the only girl in a household with four brothers was really hard. I often felt very lonely and detached. My parents had their own way of making me feel special, yet it wasn't enough to suppress my feelings. I felt that no one understood me. As long as I could remember, I always wanted a sister. While I loved my brothers, I still felt a void. I really did not have that person who I could bond with over girly stuff. You know those conversations you used to have with your sister late at night? Conversations you both still laugh about, even now as adults? That's what I'm talking about.

Although a lot of people thought I was spoiled as a child, I never felt like Daddy's little princess. You will later see how this affected my life in so many ways. I grew up with my father in the household, but I did not experience his words of affirmation. I knew my father loved me; he just never told me. Growing up without feeling the precious love from my father simply left me clueless. I constantly tried to fill a void that I felt deep inside. I was longing for fatherly love and a sense of belonging. After seeking love in the wrong places, I later made an astonishing connection: my father could not possibly give me something that he did not possess at that time. He was consumed with drugs and alcohol, and he wasn't capable of loving anyone.

Chapter 3

Abuse

As a child, I experienced physical and emotional abuse. Most families don't like to talk about the truth. But we must tell the truth so that it can free us. Healing can't take place if we don't first admit what actually happened to us. Some of the things I saw and heard as a child would make most adults go off the deep end.

For instance, when I was ten years old, I once heard gunshots coming from my parents' bedroom. My father had already told me and my brothers not to come to the door. He said that if we did, he would kill our mother. All we could do was plead with him not to harm her. We prayed for God to intervene. We heard a shot, and then another shot. We ran toward the bedroom door and started knocking very loudly. Everyone was in tears because we just knew he had taken her life.

About five minutes later, my father opened the bedroom door. To our amazement, our mother was sitting there on the bed. God heard our prayers and stopped our father from taking her life. As he hopped down the hallway, we realized that the first shot went into the ceiling and the second into his leg. I thank God for my foundation in Him. He is definitely a prayer-answering God.

God knew what I would go through as a young child and that this would only be the beginning. Throughout the years, there were constant fights and verbal abuse. Through it all, God's presence was comforting and His love covered me. It did not matter what I saw or heard; I knew that God would give me a place of peace and safety in His arms.

"And, ye fathers, provoke not your children to wrath: but bring them up in the nurture and admonition of the Lord."

Ephesians 6:4 (KJV)

Chapter 4

Teenage Years

My teenage years were very experimental. I guess you could say I was trying to figure out my identity. I did not realize it, but I had become a product of my own environment. Most of my friends and family were having fun and still attending church (and by "having fun," I mean following the crowd, smoking, drinking, and having sex).

God will allow you to go through some things to teach you a lesson, build your character, and make you stronger. I placed myself in situations where I could have been locked up in jail or worse. I really don't want to think about what the worst represents. It gives me chills just thinking about it.

There was this one time, in high school, when I was riding in the car with my cousin who was visiting from out of town. We were smoking what I thought was marijuana (at least that's what I had been told). I found out later that it was actually laced with another drug. I almost lost my life that day. The devil, desiring to sift me like wheat, told me to jump out of the speeding car. I felt invincible as I reached for the door handle. I promise you, when my hand touched the handle, God pushed it away. I reached for the handle a second time, and God pushed my hand back yet again. This happened a third time, feeling like a tug of war. My flesh was literally at war with the Holy Spirit.

"For the flesh desires what is contrary to the Spirit, and the Spirit what is contrary to the flesh. They are in conflict with each other, so that you are not to do whatever you want."

Galatians 5:17 (NIV)

I began to pray, "God, please bring me down off this high, and I will stop doing this." Finally, my flesh stopped fighting. God spared my life. I knew for certain at that point that God's hand was working in my life, and I was special to Him. That day, I experienced the peace that only God could give, even in the midst of my storm.

In my darkest dream I see many things

There is a lot of violence

It forces me to remain in silence

God! Where are you?

Can You hear my calls…lest I fall?

I have entertained strangers

Now I am facing danger

Fearful for my life yet darkness consumes me

I'm blind and I can't see

The enemy has his grips on tight

Lord! Give me the strength to fight!

I don't like the picture I see

It keeps flashing before me

Nothing beautiful but extremely UGLY!

God, have You forsaken me?

You said in Your Word that You would never leave me…

Wake me from this dream

I need to be FREE!

I will place no other God before You

I simply adore You!

I know You are capable of giving me perfect peace

No more sins of the flesh

I want what is best

Lift my feet out of the fire

It's "You" I really desire!

Beauty for ashes is what You promised me

I place my ashes at Your feet

I thank you Almighty God for restoring me

As I walk in Your BEAUTY!

Chapter 5

Adult Life

By the time I was nineteen years old, I was married with children. I know some might say that nineteen is awfully young to be married. But, I have always been that serious-minded individual who believes in commitment. Besides, by this time, I had already done everything I felt I was big and bad enough to do. It wasn't until I was about twenty-three years old that I took notice of some things.

One night, I went to a club, and as I sat there watching the crowd, I drifted off to sleep. Yep! You heard me right. There I was, sipping on a drink with the music thumping, yet I was falling asleep. God told me that night that the club life was not for me. He said I fell asleep because I was out of place. By then, I had noticed that in each phase of my life, God had showed up for me and displayed His hand. I started to understand that God would allow me to go through certain things in life because they were necessary parts of the process. That night, my desire to go to the club faded away.

As I grew in the Word, God began to pull me closer to Him. He continued to show His unfailing love for me. He knew what was best for me, and not only did He take things away from me, but He also replaced them with things that added value to my life. This is how God works–we may not understand everything that He does, yet things always work for our good. This reminds me of one of my favorite scriptures:

"We are assured and know that [God being a partner in their labor] all things work together and are [fitting into a plan] for good to and for those who love God and are called according to [His] design and purpose."

Romans 8:28 (AMPC)

During this process, I lost family, friends, houses, credit, businesses, marriages….I could go on, but you get the picture. I would often ask God, "Why me?" but then He would say, "Why not you?"

Consider your own story. God has equipped you from the very beginning, and He will not put any more on you than you can bear. If I had never experienced falling down, how could I help anyone get up? Every single thing that happens in life happens for a reason. It is up to us to learn and apply these lessons to our lives. The problem is that, a lot of the time, we get stuck on another person's opinion of us. Don't be afraid to make changes that will work out for your good. Being a God-pleaser is more important than being a people-pleaser. When you please God and totally trust Him with your life, things begin to work out. Trust me, I know. I've done too many things on my own (and that, my friend, is why those things didn't work out).

Everything I lost, God has replaced. I am not going to tell you that it was easy, because I had to work my faith. When I fell, it was hard. I'm not talking about just a little superficial wound. Some of my wounds probably would have driven other people crazy. Some wounds were deep cuts in my soul. Some even crushed my spirit. But when I realized that I was on the winning team and that the fight was fixed, it was amazing. You may be thinking, *All I have to do is stay in the ring and tough it out?* Yes, that is exactly what I am telling you. Don't tap out of life, simply give it to God.

You can trust God to do everything He said He would do. God has replaced the friends and family who I lost along the way with more people. "Lost" does not mean only physically in death, but also mentally and emotionally. You see, I have had people check out on me simply because I decided to follow Jesus all the way. To me, it was one of the best decisions I ever made. It was positively life-changing. You would think that they would be happy for me, but quite the contrary. By following Jesus, I caused others to take an honest look at their lives, and some were not ready to change. Resentment set in, so they checked out. I realized that this was a trick of the enemy, and that I had to continue to trust the process. God placed had people in my life to help me grow spiritually. Now, I often pray that He would send people to my sons to help guide each of them back to Christ. I am a witness to the fact that God is married to the backslider.

Sometimes, we think that we have done so much wrong in our life that God can't use us. It does not matter what you've done. God is a forgiving God. He never leaves us. And although we may leave Him, He receives us back with open arms. If you bring your children up in the nurture and admonition of God, they will be alright, even if they go astray.

When I lost the house I had built from the ground up due to foreclosure, I was crushed. I was going through a divorce at the time and could no longer afford my house. What I came to realize was that a house is not always a home. When you allow the enemy to come into your home and wreak havoc, it is no longer your safe haven. I am thankful to God that I have never been a materialistic person. Don't get me wrong; I like nice things, but those things don't define me as a person. What bothered me the most about the foreclosure was the fact that I had put so much hard work into getting the house, but I was not able to keep it. Here's a message for you: if God blesses you with a house and you lose it, He is more than able to do it again. God has blessed me with another house, and there are still more houses and land to come.

When my credit was tore up and I had to file for bankruptcy, God was there. My business, which was once thriving, became very slow. I felt like my whole world was crumbling before my eyes. When you talk about being made uncomfortable, well, this was the moment. One thing about this was that I never gave up, even though calamity was on every corner. I continued to keep God first, and I was more determined than ever. Some of the wounds in our lives are self-inflicted. You question yourself over and over again, how did I get here? God's answer is always the same. Trust the process, because you are a winner.

Women of faith are filled with strength and power

We know how to get a prayer through every hour.

We are clothed in praise and worship and our tongues are filled with grace

We recognize our positions and how to run the race.

We arise each morning ready for war; God has brought us thus far

He carries us through the fire, disappointments, and pain

We adore our heavenly Father and await our eternal gain.

Believing beyond what our eyes might see, we place our trust in God totally.

There is a pressing in our spirits to do the work of the Lord

Despite the obstacles that are thrown our way, we just continue to pray

Women of faith believe that somehow our God will make a way.

Sometimes we might take a bruising, slapped with confusion and kicked with

depression

The enemy tries to teach us a lesson.

He weakens us to what might seem like the point of defeat

Now it's really time to fight! We can't tap out!

We just lie prostrate at the Savior's feet.

As we know when we draw closer to God, He draws even closer to us

We empty ourselves and He fills our cup

There is nothing less than VICTORY when we come up.

We have our victory stance again

We know that the fight is fixed, and in the end "WE WIN"!!!!

Adult Life

Chapter 6

Just Be Yourself

T here are many people who secretly covet others, but the Bible tells us not to be envious of others. No matter how hard you may try, you can never be that other person. God has made each and every one of us in His own image. We all have been given gifts and talents to share with the world. We are all divine creatures with unique souls.

"You shall not covet your neighbor's house. You shall not covet your neighbor's wife, or his male or female servant, his ox or donkey, or anything that belongs to your neighbor."

Exodus 20:17 (NIV)

Someone once confessed to me that they were jealous of me. Shockingly, these words came from someone whom I really admired. She was also my sister in Christ. We weren't just co-workers, but friends. My first question was, "Why?" I could not understand what would make her feel this way. She explained that she noticed how people clung to me during conversation. She said they simply did not gravitate to her in the same manner.

She also told me that she owed me an apology for bashing my name among our clients and co-workers at work (this goes to show you that jealousy will bring out the worst in people. It is like entering a danger zone). Although I was hurt by her actions, I realized that the Holy Spirit had convicted her spirit and caused her to do the right thing. I know that it takes a lot to admit your shortcomings. We all have fallen short of the glory of God at some point. The Word of God tells us the righteous will fall, but they get back up.

I simply told my friend to just be herself. People can tell when you are not being genuine. In order to attract friends, you must first prove yourself to be friendly. I am a naturally friendly person who meets no strangers. When you take your mind off others and focus more on God, He'll show you your natural abilities. What He has for you is distinctly for you, because no one else has your unique qualities.

Chapter 7

Walking in Unforgiveness

There was a time when I knew I had it all together. I was
back in church serving God and His people. Everything
was going great (at least so I thought) until one particular
Sunday afternoon. My pastor was preaching a sermon
called "Unforgiveness," and it was as if he was talking directly to
me. I couldn't figure out why, but God placed my father in my
spirit. Meanwhile, I was trying to convince God that there was
nothing wrong with my father and me. When the sermon was
over, my pastor did an altar call for those who needed to come up
for prayer and deliverance. I was completely drowning in my tears.
I was the first to rush up the aisle for prayer. God had shown me
that I had only forgiven my father with words, but my heart was
far from forgiveness.

I realized that I had suppressed my feelings so much, that they
were buried deeply within me. I believed that if I never thought or

talked about the pain, then it would eventually go away. After all, I still talked with my father occasionally. He had abandoned our family and ran off with another woman when I was in high school. I remember coming home from school and my mother telling me that he left and was not coming back home. I was devastated to hear this news, and I was at a point in my life when I really needed him. Many years had gone by, but I hadn't realized that my life was in danger because I was walking in unforgiveness.

During the sermon, my pastor said that you have to completely forgive others so that God will forgive you of your sins. I thank God for exposing what was hidden in my heart. It is indeed possible to hold on to something without realizing it. For this reason, we should ask God to search our hearts and cleanse us of all unrighteousness. In that moment, I immediately repented of my sin and asked God to forgive me. God spoke to me and said, "You must go to your father today and ask for his forgiveness." I was overwhelmed with a sense of urgency, so I obeyed God.

As soon as service was over, I made a beeline to my father's home. He was so surprised to see me standing there as he opened the door. I felt a lump in my throat, but I finally got the words to come out. I apologized to my father for not forgiving him for the pain he had caused our entire family. I told him that I loved him (now you know this was God, because my father was still living with the same woman at the time. When I tell you the Holy Spirit gives you power!). I then gave him a hug and left.

Shortly after my encounter with my father, he became very ill. He moved back in with my mother, and she took care of him until he passed away. I am so glad that I followed the voice of God that Sunday and went to him to get things right. The Lord knew what was ahead and wanted to prepare me for it. If God had not intervened in this situation, I might have missed the opportunity for closure, and most importantly, forgiveness.

I challenge you today; if you have unforgiveness in your heart for someone who hurt you, take a moment now to make things right, before it is too late. Let us hold fast to what the Word of God tells us:

"Strive to live in peace with everybody and pursue that consecration and holiness without which no one will [ever] see the Lord."

Hebrews 12:14 (AMPC)

Is there someone who hurt you in the past or perhaps disrespected you in the worst way possible? Did you really forgive their actions? If God placed a name or face in your spirit, then that is the person you must forgive. You must go to that person and make things right. I know you are probably saying, "Well, I am not the one who hurt them." I thought the same thing. Believe it or not, forgiveness is for you, not the other person.

"And whenever you stand praying, if you have anything against anyone, forgive him and let it drop (leave it, let it go), in order that your Father Who is in heaven may also forgive you your [own] failings and shortcomings and let them drop."

Mark 11:25 (AMPC)

You see, sometimes we can hold up God's blessings in our lives because we willingly choose to struggle with issues that He has already rescued us from. I know the struggle is real, but so is our God! Say this prayer with me:

God, I come before you, right now, asking you to please search my heart. If there is anything within me that does not line up with your Word, please take it away from me. Please forgive me for not forgiving others. I ask that you give me peace with everyone who has done me wrong. Create in me a clean heart, God, and renew a right spirit within me.

It is in Jesus' name I pray. AMEN.

Chapter 8

God, Where Are You?

Have you ever found yourself in a desert season? By this, I mean not feeling God's presence in your life? Sometimes, we can get so busy in life that we can't feel God's presence. It's not that His presence is not there, but our presence is absent. God desires a completely faithful relationship with His children. God will never leave us nor forsake us. When we get too far away from Him, He has a way of isolating us to get our attention. Usually at this point, He has spoken to us several times. We may not have been listening because we've been too busy or too tired.

There was a time when I was a member of the praise team, the choir, the dance ministry, a community volunteer organization, and a Bible class. I sang with our praise team at the eight o'clock and eleven o'clock services. I was also working twelve hours per day, six days per week. God had to slow me down with all the things I had going on, because I was too tired to give Him myself. In my mind, I was thinking that everything was good in His sight. After all, I was still taking care of my family. None of this mattered, though, if I was not in His presence.

Then, I was taken out of work due to a major surgery. This surgery would require at least six weeks of recovery time. And it was major in more than just one way. When my surgeon went in, he discovered an additional problem. I was told afterwards that I required additional repairs, which ended up causing difficulties once I returned home. I could not urinate on my own, so I had to use a catheter whenever my bladder was full. This process went on for about one week, which really concerned my doctor. He said that all of my bodily functions should return after a few days, but I was now included in the one percent of people who did not heal in the expected time frame. Needless to say, I became very nervous and began to think the absolute worst. The process was already very painful, so I just couldn't imagine what I would do if this became something permanent. I just could not believe this was happening to me. I prayed to God for my healing and began to listen to praise and worship music morning and night. I needed to know that God was still there. Ultimately, I knew this was a time that God was allowing because He was trying to tell me something.

During this time, I would sit on the toilet and press down on my bladder, over and over again, with hopes of feeling even the smallest drop of urine release on its own accord. After numerous attempts without anything happening, I really began to cry out to the Lord. I was so desperate to get a breakthrough. I asked God to please help me. I continued to seek His face as I continued to press and push down, over and over again. Suddenly, I just broke out in a crazy praise and finally felt one drop come out. God said to me, "Now, see how desperate you were and how you continued to press? That is how I want you to be when it comes to seeking my face in my Word." All I could say was, "Yes, Lord," as I sat there in tears.

See, we can get so busy doing the things of God that we neglect Him. I was in a desert season because I wasn't spending quality time with Him. I was in the house of God consistently yet too tired to nurture our relationship. A wise man once said, "We owe God at least two hours and forty minutes per day." It is God who actually blesses us with twenty-four hours each day anyway.

God, Where Are You?

Chapter 9

Meaningful Purpose

I have always been a very hard worker, and some might consider me a workaholic. But as much as I loved my job as a cosmetologist, I began to feel a little burned out during a particular season. It was sometime around 1993 when I decided to get another job through a temp agency, just to try something different. I started working at a mortgage company. Immediately, my supervisor and I just clicked. It was as if we had known each other for years. We were able to talk and really get to know each other well. I'm sure my co-workers did not understand our relationship, because we stuck together like glue. We became close like sisters, and even I could not understand it, because this was my supervisor.

One day, my supervisor happened to come into the restroom as I was leaving. I could tell that something was not quite right with her, so I asked her if she was okay. She asked me to pray with her. I did not know why she was upset, but the Spirit did, so I began to pray. After praying, I asked if she had a relationship with God. She told me that she had backslid from the things of God but desired to come back to the household of faith. She just didn't know if she was ready. At this time, she was occasionally attending church and trying to find her way back.

Then, it all started coming together. God did not bring me to this new job because I wanted something different at the time. He brought me there on assignment. God had a meaningful purpose in mind. I went back to my desk and said a silent prayer. God spoke to me and said, "I need you to draw her heart back to me." As time went by, we started to hang out more and more. There were times when she would come to my desk and ask me to pray right there in the open. Sometimes, she would even ask me to sing a song to help brighten up her day. God had me minister to her every chance I could, and the Holy Ghost led me. One day, she came to me with the most beautiful smile on her face to share what happened the day before. She had given her life back to Christ! This is a day I will never forget. All I could do was give God praise for all He had done. I had been hired permanently by this time, and I knew this is where God wanted me to be.

Shortly after giving her life to Christ, the company's workload began to slow down and they started layoffs. God later told me that He wanted me to return to my business, because my business was my ministry. It wasn't until this season of life that I understood that He had already given me the platform to do his bidding and to draw souls to Him. It's like my eyes were opened and I could now see clearly. From that day forward, I have not looked at my business the same way. I realize that it is not just a business, but also a ministry.

My business is where I set the atmosphere for greatness; I pray, preach, teach, sing, and shout. God gets all the glory out of my life. What are you doing to bring glory to God? You don't have to have the title of minister to be a minister. Use whatever platform or opportunity you have to win a soul for God.

Meaningful Purpose

Chapter 10

God Has a Sense of Humor

When I was pregnant with my youngest son, I enrolled in a Method of Teaching Class. I did not have many maternity clothes at the time, and one day I was running late because I could not find anything to wear. Well, the class was located on the other side of town. I panicked because the class was fast-paced and I did not want to miss any instructions. Nothing seemed to be working for me. Finally, I found an outfit that fit right. I put it on and quickly ran out the door, heading towards my car. A small voice then told me to look down. I looked down, and all my cleavage was out. Now at this point, I felt overwhelmed because I knew there was nothing else for me to wear to class. Lord knows I didn't have any safety pins. If only I could find just one, maybe I could still make it to class on time. So I said, "Lord, please help me!"

Then, a small voice told me to go to the trunk. I stood there with this crazy look on my face. Again, I heard the voice tell me to go to my trunk and look inside. At that time, I had so much junk in my trunk, I couldn't imagine why on earth God would send me there. Out of obedience, I started looking through my trunk. All I knew was that I trusted Him.

There I was, outside, rambling through all this stuff in my trunk without even knowing what I was supposed to find there. When I got to the bottom of all that stuff, I found a yellow folder, so I picked it up. The folder had a safety pin attached to the back. It was sitting there, waiting for me to find it. We serve an amazing God with a great sense of humor. Who else could have done that?

God said to me, "You asked for my help, and you had enough faith to believe that I would help. If I bless you with the minute things, how much more could I bless you with the big things that you ask of me?" I promise you, immediately my hands went up in praise and His precious Spirit was all over me. I know the Holy Spirit did the driving for me that day, because I praised God all the way to class. I was able to pin up my blouse and make it to class on time.

When we ask God for something, we must believe that it is already done. It does not matter how crazy it might seem. When you don't quite understand, just trust God's voice. Every time I think about this testimony, even today, I still laugh and give Him praise.

Chapter 11

Out of the Mouth of Babes

God will use anyone to get a word to you. There was a time when He used my baby girl to speak to me. During this time, I was a single parent and dealing with a lot on my own. My oldest son had been getting into trouble at school, and the phone calls were coming in daily. I had prayed about it, taken things away from him, spanked him, and even took him to the altar for deliverance. Nothing seemed to work.

One Sunday, we were in church (I believe it was Easter Sunday). I remember praising God until I tore my hem from my maxi skirt while dancing in the Spirit. My spirit had been so heavy because I had allowed depression to set in. I was determined not to leave church the same. I got my breakthrough, but as soon as I walked out of the service, the enemy was waiting at the door. My children and I walked towards the car and got in. I sat there and cried uncontrollable tears. I couldn't understand why, but I could not pull myself together enough to drive away. The children began to ask me what was wrong. I still could not speak. My baby girl, who was only about eight years old, looked at me and said, "God said he will be all right!" It was as if God Himself was speaking to me. It was such a short phrase, yet it was so profound. Immediately in my spirit, I felt something release. I grabbed my baby girl and held her tightly, thanking her for being obedient to God. I heard God speak through her, and at that moment I knew it would be all right. God had stopped the fiery darts of the enemy, and He assured me that He had my oldest son covered.

My baby girl doesn't remember this happening. I shared the incident with her recently, and she had no recollection of the event, but I thank God for using her that day. Even to this day, she prays for me and always has a word for me. Never dismiss what a little child has to say—it just might be God speaking. My oldest son is thirty-five years old and has been through a lot, but God did not allow the enemy to kill him. I had to trust God all the way and believe what He said.

"At that time the disciples came up and asked Jesus, who then is [really] the greatest in the kingdom of heaven? And He called a little child to Himself and put him in the midst of them, and said, truly I say to you, unless you repent (change, turn about) and become like little children [trusting, lowly, loving, forgiving], you can never enter the kingdom of heaven [at all]. Whoever will humble himself therefore and become like this little child [trusting, lowly, loving, forgiving] is greatest in the kingdom of heaven. And whoever receives and accepts and welcomes one little child like this for My sake and in My name receives and accepts and welcomes Me."

Matthew 18:1-5 (AMPC)

Out of the Mouth of Babes

Chapter 12

When You Lose Your Mind

I have to laugh to myself because I know what you are thinking: Lose my mind? I felt the same way when I heard this topic in church one Sunday morning. All I knew was, I wasn't trying to lose my mind. But when it was all said and done, I was ready to lose my mind, because it meant gaining the mind of Christ.

As human beings, we can have jacked-up mindsets. We sometimes allow our feelings to get in the way of our thinking. The fact of the matter is, our feelings have little to do with having the right mindsets. Our brains process the information that they receive and send messages back to our bodies. We think and experience emotions with our brains. Some of these emotions include anger, lust, and pain, just to name a few. The enemy likes to use our minds as playgrounds, because he knows that is where our thought processes begins. If he can control our minds, then he has us right where he wants us.

Our experiences in life can cause us to have negative mindsets, especially when we are consumed with pain and disappointment. These things can cloud our minds and our capacities for reasoning. But when we take on the mind of Jesus Christ, we can make great decisions. God has infinite wisdom and is waiting for us to take on His mindset. Here are a few scriptures to meditate on:

"And be not conformed to this world: but be ye transformed by the renewing of your mind, that ye may prove what is that good, and acceptable, and perfect, will of God."

Romans 12:2 (KJV)

"Let this mind be in you, which was also in Christ Jesus."

Philippians 2:5 (KJV)

"For God hath not given us the spirit of fear; but of power, and of love, and of
a sound mind."

2 Timothy 1:7 (KJV)

"Finally, brethren, whatsoever things are true,
Whatsoever things are honest
Whatsoever things are just
Whatsoever things are pure
Whatsoever thing are lovely
Whatsoever things are of good report
If there be any virtue, and if there be any praise, think on these things."

Philippians 4:8 (KJV)

The more we take on the mind of Christ, the more we are able to be optimistic, to love the unlovable, and to display the fruits of the Spirit. Jesus Christ has set an excellent example for us to follow. Reading more of God's Word transforms our minds daily to live more spiritual lives.

There was a time when I would get upset if someone said they did not like me. I would actually stay up at night wondering why. Now that I have taken on the mindset of Christ and have become more spiritual, it does not bother me. What does matter is how God feels about me. I just pray for the person and let it go.

Once you become serious about the things of God, your whole atmosphere changes along with your mind. The enemy no longer has the power to keep you up at night worrying about things you can't control.

Chapter 13

Look for Reasons

I t is so easy for someone to come up with an excuse when they don't want to do something. I always say that people do what they want to do. The problem is that, when we are facing something unfamiliar to us, fear sets in, making it easy to say no. As we know, God has not given us the spirit of fear. We must step out in faith and know that God has already equipped us for the task at hand.

As I told you before, being in front of an audience was something I was forced to do as a child, so I readily volunteered for such tasks. But to be honest, I never really liked being in front of people. It's true. I'm a little shy when it comes to all the attention placed on me. I think it's because I was teased so much as a child, and I did not like the way it made me feel. For a long time, I actually had low self-esteem because of the negativity that surrounded me.

But I have learned that it is not about what you feel. When it comes to God, we must place our feelings aside. Everything we do in life should represent Him. Even now, as an adult, when I'm asked to sing a song, write a poem, or read an announcement, I still get nervous. These are some of the things that I know I can do well, but it does not change the way I feel. I realize it is God who gives me these abilities anyway. I repeated this scripture over and over until it stuck like glue:

"For God hath not given us the spirit of fear; but of power, and of love, and of a sound mind,"

2 Timothy 1:7 (KJV)

If everything that we do is based on how we feel, we might not ever step out in faith because we will always find an excuse to justify why we can't do something.

Whenever another year is about to arrive, my first lady always asks me, "What are you looking for God to do in the new year?" I often reply, "To give me more faith and boldness." I don't want to hesitate or come up with an excuse when it comes to doing what I know He has called me to do. I have everything I need in His Word. My pastor spoke on this topic one Sunday. He said that whenever you start to think of an excuse for not doing something, find a reason to do it.

"Only fear the Lord and serve Him faithfully with all your heart; for consider how great are the things He has done for you."

1 Samuel 12:24 (AMPC)

"Whatever may be your task, work at it heartily (from the soul), as [something done] for the Lord and not for men."

Colossians 3:23 (AMPC)

"I give thanks to Him who has granted me [the needed] strength and made me able [for this], Christ Jesus our Lord, because He has judged and counted me faithful and trustworthy, appointing me to [this stewardship of] the ministry."

1 Timothy 1:12 (AMPC)

"I have strength for all things in Christ who empowers me. [I am ready for anything and equal to anything through Him who infuses inner strength into me; I am self-sufficient in Christ's sufficiency]."

Philippians 4:13 (AMPC)

You will not have to look far to find a reason to do the thing that is required. The next time you find yourself searching for an excuse, pull out this book and repeat these scriptures. Allow them to bless you real good.

God of mercy, God of grace

Help me to make it through this day.

Strengthen me, O God, to go forth and do Your work;

It's not about me but about Your church.

I must deny flesh and concentrate on You

Give me the wisdom to do whatever You would have me to do.

You have given me another day to live

Yet another day to strive and to give people

What you have planted inside.

I will tell of Your goodness everywhere I go

The closer I get to You, the more I have to pour.

I take delight in placing a smile on Your face

God, help me to draw a lost soul toward You today!

Chapter 14

Who Do You Say God Is?

od is the creator of all things. He is holy and perfect in all His ways. He is omnipresent, omniscient, and omnipotent. This means that God is everywhere at the same time, all-knowing, and all-powerful. He is as big or as small as your faith allows Him to be. And my faith was strengthened during childbirth.

The birthing process leaves me speechless. Who else could take credit for such a miraculous encounter but God? Certainly, no one I know could even come close. When I think about how a man and woman come together, and nine months later give birth to someone who looks like them, it is simply amazing. Just knowing that God blesses us with the ability to reproduce should convert any non-believer. I sometimes sit in awe of this entire process.

God is everything to me! There is no problem too big for my God to solve. I talk to God about the smallest things in life because He is my friend. He knows me better than I know myself, and I don't have to worry about Him telling my business to anybody.

When I was twelve, God kept me from having a nervous breakdown because I thought my mother was going to leave me. I sat on the floor with my face pressed up against the stereo speaker, crying and begging God not to allow my father to take her life. By this time, I had seen and heard too much and I did not know how to process it. I never told my mother about this because I did not want to burden her. God was there to preserve my mind. God is a deliverer! Hallelujah!

When I had my first child at seventeen years old, God was there for me. He did not turn His back on me because I made a mistake. Although my parents were disappointed, they did not turn their backs on me, neither. God gave me the strength to endure everything that came along with a teenage pregnancy, including the looks of ridicule, the laughs, and the whispers. God is my Rock and Refuge!

"Therefore, [there is] now no condemnation (no adjudging guilty of wrong) for those who are in Christ Jesus, who live [and] walk not after the dictates flesh, but after the dictates of the Spirit. For the law of the spirit of life [which is] in Christ Jesus [the law of our new being] has freed me from the law of sin and of death."

Romans 8:1-2 (AMPC)

Chapter 15

When You Know God is Speaking

For the first time in my life, I have found myself experiencing a worldwide pandemic. Covid-19 forced us into isolation, and our church officially closed. So one Sunday morning, my husband and I sat down together to watch our pastor's weekly sermon online. After listening to the message for that day, my husband began to play gospel music videos.

I sat there, glued to my seat, pondering the message. It was entitled "The Enemy Doesn't Want Me to Succeed." My pastor said that although we were in midst of the pandemic, we still had to get the Word out and that our mission was essential. As I pondered this, Tasha Cobbs Leonard's song, "For Your Glory," began to play. The song really started to minister to my husband and me, and we began to praise and worship God (it's such a beautiful thing to have a husband who is sold out for God and knows how to submit to His presence). God then spoke to me and said that He needed me to go to my baby girl's house to give her a hug. He also said to go to my mother's house and anoint her with oil and pray for her.

Well, it wasn't in my plans to go anywhere that day, but God had a different plan for me. Immediately, I got out of my seat. I told my husband what God had said to me. My husband wanted me to drive to my mother's house first, because of the distance. I told him that's not what God said to me, and that I had to be obedient. When you know God is speaking to you and giving instructions, you must follow His specific directions. It could be a matter of life or death, and obedience is better than sacrifice.

When I stepped outside to get into my car, I noticed it was raining. People who know me are aware of the fact that I don't like driving in the rain. But I would do anything for God's glory. My mission was set before me.

I called my daughter to let her know I would be coming by for a few minutes, and she was elated. When I arrived at her house, I grabbed her and gave her a hug. I told her that God had sent me over to embrace her. She told me that she definitely needed a hug and she knew it was God who sent me. She asked me to pray for her, and of course I did. She and her husband had to make a life-altering decision. He had been offered a job in another state, and they would have to relocate if he accepted the position. She had been struggling with the thought of relocation, but she was very proud of her husband's accomplishment. God told me to share two scriptures with her. As I walked out the door, I knew in my spirit that all would be well. The next day, it was made official, and God won again. What the enemy meant for evil, God turned around for her good.

My next assignment was at my mother's house. God had already made it possible for my mother and me to be alone. My mother had been having bodily pain for two weeks, and nothing she did would relieve it. We read some healing scriptures together and made them very personal. Let me tell you, the Word works. After we prayed, I began to anoint the body parts that she pointed out with oil. I prayed for her healing to take place. The very next day, she was feeling better. I could hear the difference in her voice and knew that she was no longer suffering with the same level of pain she previously had. What a mighty God we serve!

"Heal me, O Lord, and I shall be healed; save me, and I shall be saved, for You are my praise."

Jeremiah 17:14 (AMPC)

"Is anyone among you sick? He should call in the church elders (the spiritual guides). And they should pray over him, anointing him with oil in the Lord's name. And the prayer [that is] of faith will save him who is sick, and the Lord will restore him; and if he has committed sins, he will be forgiven."

James 5:14-15 (AMPC)

"Therefore confess your sins to each other and pray for each other so that you may be healed. The prayer of a righteous person is powerful and effective."

James 5:16 (NIV)

Chapter 16

I Don't Look Like
What I've Been Through

When I think about my life and everything that I have been through, I am really grateful. I am so happy that when I was out in the world sinning, God didn't call my number. No one knows when they will leave this earth, but I am glad to still be here. I can recall so many circumstances when God intervened to save my life.

The first thing that comes to mind is when I was a teenager. As I mentioned previously, I had tried drugs. Not only did I experiment with marijuana, but there was also a time when I snorted cocaine and took a microdot pill. Now, that only happened once, but sometimes all it takes is one time to overdose and possibly lose your life.

Secondly, I think about the time I went into a movie theatre packing a pistol and marijuana in my purse for a friend. If the police had caught me, do you think my friend would have told the truth? Now, if that wasn't bad enough, I later started selling drugs for that same friend. What was I thinking? BUT GOD!!!

Thirdly, I think about the many surgeries that I have had throughout my life. I believe I've had about nine or ten. God brought me through them all without major complications. The one that scared me the most was the thyroidectomy (the thought of the doctor cutting my throat was terrifying). I have always loved to sing, so I asked God to please save my voice throughout the process. I can't hit some of my top soprano notes like I used to, but I can still minister with song.

In each of these circumstances, God showed up for me. I always knew it was His hand at work, ever since He kept my mind sound as a little girl. He would not allow the enemy to take my sanity or my life. He saved me from myself. He knew my future, and He needed me to show up for it. He had plans for me, even when I went under the knife. There might have been complications, but He turned what might have been major issues into minor ones. He needed me, just like I needed Him, because I had to live to tell of His goodness. His love for me is unconditional. God has kept me from a road of self-destruction and self-inflicted wounds. Who would not serve a God like that?

"I shall not die, but live, and declare the works of the Lord."

Psalms 118:17 (KJV)

For those of you who might share similar testimonies about the dark places you have experienced in your life, God forgives you. The problem is, many of us don't forgive ourselves and feel unworthy of His love. God wants to love you through your pain and deliver you from evil. He knows who He created you to be, and it is never too late to come to Him (or in some cases come back to Him).

It is because God loved me so much that He never gave up on me, no matter what craziness I got myself into at the time. The very things that I had to endure in life helped me become the person who I am today. Some may look at me and never know that I've have been through so much. God will preserve you and bring you forth in His timing. Today I can truly say that, no matter the circumstances I find myself in, I know God is there with me. When I come through the other side, I know I will look good. It's all good because it's all God. I am forever grateful for all He has done for me.

Lord you covered me.

You have healed my heart.

You kept me from all danger that would have torn me apart.

I know this one thing

Your Word is true!

You didn't leave me nor forsake me, that's why I love You!

You are so faithful to me, so I must be faithful to You.

I will continue to read Your word and bless Your name.

I will testify to others of how Your love never changes.

You are the "God of Heaven" and "Spirit of Truth"

Keep me close, dear Lord

So when it's my time, I will go home with You!

Closing Thoughts

I love God with all my heart. I want to encourage you to keep relying, trusting, and adhering to the Word of God. We all have fallen short of the glory of God. Whenever you feel like giving up on life, just remember God's investment in you. I believe we all can look back at some points in our lives and see how the hand of God has delivered us many times. His track record speaks well for itself. No matter what you have done in life, it's never too late to get things right with our Father.

You do not have to be a product of your environment. I know there are some people, like me, who've had to endure a lot and don't quite understand it. Everything that you go through in life is not necessarily for you alone. You must share your testimony with others to help them believe that God is who He says He is. If I had not gone through my tests in life, then how would I be capable of telling you of God's goodness and how He is more than able to see you through any situation?

God takes us through some things so we can get to know Him. I can tell you He is a healer because He has healed me. I can tell you that He is a way maker because He has made a way for me. I can tell you that He loves you, because the Word tells me that He is love. He shows us His love each day we awaken and see the dawning of a new day.

God speaks to us in many ways. His Holy Spirit leads and guides us daily. I encourage you— when God tugs at your heart, let Him in. You have tried things your way. Open up and let Him in so He can change your life today.

Acknowledgements

I am blessed with a loving mother, Patricia Strother, who cared enough for me to introduce me to Jesus Christ. You are the epitome of a great mother and friend. You have always been by my side, praying for me and encouraging me. God bless you for all your dedication, love, and support.

I praise God for my devoted husband and best friend, Michael Wilson. Thank you for being so understanding, selfless, and supportive. You have cheered me on, right from the start. Thank you for believing in me and being my biggest fan.

Finally, thank you to all my family and friends who have given words of encouragement throughout this process. I solicit your continued prayers and support.

Acknowledgements

Made in the USA
Columbia, SC
31 March 2021

35391853R00041